Offshore on the Southern

The Isle of Wight railways in the 1950s and 1960s

Anthony Burges

Colourpoint Books

Offshore On The Southern

Dedicated to the Isle of Wight Steam Railway and its dedicated band of volunteers who have so successfully kept alive the spirit of a lost but fondly remembered railway for future generations.

First Edition
First Impression

Designed by Colourpoint Books
Printed by ColourBooks Ltd

ISBN 978 1 904242 80 2

Colourpoint Books
Colourpoint House
Jubilee Business Park
21 Jubilee Road
Newtownards
County Down
Northern Ireland
BT23 4YH
Tel: 028 9182 0505
Fax: 028 9182 1900
E-mail: info@colourpoint.co.uk
Web-site: www.colourpoint.co.uk

After an initial period as a 'mourner' in the fifties at branch line funerals in the UK and Ireland, Tony pursued studies at Southampton University followed by graduate school at Northwestern University, Chicago. His subsequent career in the Canadian government as Transport Policy Advisor in the Department of Finance , Director General, Grain Transportation & Handling, and subsequently Deputy Executive Director, Australian Railway Research & Development Organization earned him the sobriquet of 'Mr Branchline' among his colleagues. Retiring recently from a Washington DC based firm of transportation consultants he is now devoting his time to writing railway books in Ottawa.

Unless otherwise credited all photographs are by the author.

Front cover: No 26 *Whitwell* traverses Ryde Pier with a Cowes train in July 1964. The tracks in the foreground are those of the Ryde Pier Tramway. Pier Head station is visible in the background.

Rear cover: No 25 *Godshill* leaves Ashley with a Ryde Pier Head-Cowes train in July 1964.

Introduction

The writers first awareness of 'the island' began with the passage of the impressive green liveried twelve car Waterloo–Portsmouth Harbour 4COR electric units, as they passed Malden (now New Malden) station at what seemed like high speed with their front end vestibule connection swaying rhythmically back and forth accompanied by a spectacular display of arcing from the conductor shoes and third rail, plus the high pitched piping sound of their whistle. These trains, carrying headcode 8, followed the route to the naval garrison of Portsmouth and the sea but were also a link to ferry connections for an island with its own geographically separate and surprisingly complex rail system.

The 4 CORs had style, a comfortable ride, on board refreshments and offered a scenic journey across Surrey and Hampshire. The frequent and well patronized ferries that plied between Portsmouth Harbour and Ryde Pier Head added an exotic touch with a short cruise of half an hour or so duration that provided fascinating glimpses of the abundance of naval and merchant shipping in the Spithead and a welcome breath of sea air.

But the real fun began on arrival at Ryde Pier Head where the hoards of holidaymakers were disgorged onto the station concourse, only to meet the outgoing crowds returning to the mainland. Summer season peak traffic on Saturdays resulted in as many as fifty to seventy thousand passengers being relatively smoothly and routinely handled at Pier Head. The public address system efficiently guided those destined for Ryde Espanade and Southern Vectis bus connections to the unpretentious, yet efficient, Pier tramway, whilst the railway platforms were thronged with families rushing to secure seats in clean, if elderly, non corridor carriages destined for the holiday resorts such as Sandown, Shanklin and Ventnor as well as other parts of the Island.

The sounds were unforgettable. The station announcer's strong regional accent brought a sense of distinctiveness and hint of mystery to such destinations as Cowes, and his instructions regarding the necessity of changing at Brading for Bembridge and Newport for Freshwater hinted at further delights lurking in remoter parts of the island rail network. One had undoubtedly reached the portal of a slightly foreign railway empire. The general hubbub was punctuated by the impatient panting of Westinghouse brake pumps on fussy little Adams O2 tank locomotives which obviously reflected an unusual measure of tender loving care right down to their resplendent brass nameplates proclaiming their local allegiance to the Island. Even their strange sounding whistles, reminiscent of the LMS, differentiated them from their mainland counterparts on the Southern. The station staff and train crews were friendly and seemed dedicated to getting travellers to their destinations as quickly as possible. It seemed as though the continuous procession of crowded trains was straining the Pier Head terminus to its limits. All this contrasted with the accumulated neglect and grime of much of the mainland network. The island was truly a place to get away from it all.

The railways of the island, even though they were carrying an estimated total of more than three million passengers in 1951, were nonetheless performing a secondary role to the noisy vibrating Bristol buses of Southern Vectis that laboured mightily up and down the hills of the island's tortuous road network. Overall, the door to door convenience of the bus service attracted the allegiance of more than seventeen million island travelers each year. The railways came into their own with the massive seasonal surges of visitors who flocked to the island on summer saturdays. By contrast the winter was a period of relative calm and tranquility on the island system including the Ryde–Ventnor line.

The latin expression 'multum in parvo' aptly described the railways, for in a hilly landscape measuring a maximum of 23 miles from east to west, by 13 miles from north to south, there existed a total of fifty-four and a half route miles of railway which served thirty three stations, of which all but four were staffed, plus two halts restricted to workmen's traffic. Loco sheds at Ryde St Johns and Newport were home to a fleet of twenty-three Adams Class O2 0-4-4 tanks built for the L&SWR between 1889 and 1892 and four ex-LB&SCR Stroudley Class E1 0-6-0 tanks dating from 1878 to 1881. Similarly the passenger rolling stock was of exclusively pre-grouping (1923) vintage built for the LB&SCR and SE&CR. From the early days, the three original constituent companies – the Isle of Wight Railway, the Isle of Wight Central Railway and the Freshwater, Yarmouth and Newport Railway – relied heavily for motive power and rolling stock on 'hand-me-downs' from mainland railways, a factor which contributed to a rich and varied history which has received detailed attention elsewhere (see selected bibliography).

In essence, by 1950 the island system was a sprightly and well maintained operating museum. To add to its distinctiveness there was something faintly colonial about the way it was administered, with day to day management delegated to a Special Assistant for the Isle of Wight located at Newport station.

The economy of the Isle of Wight has been traditionally dominated by agriculture and tourism so that freight was always overshadowed by passenger traffic, on the rail system. In 1951 the total return freight workings on the island ranged from forty-one to fifty-seven per week according to demand. Waterborne traffic to and from the mainland, including the all important loco coal supply, was handled at Medina Wharf located on the Medina River south of Cowes, while the wharf at St Helens, on the Bembridge branch, had declined in importance and fulfilled a lesser role. A skeleton service of one return freight working on weekdays linked Ryde St Johns to Newport, Bembridge and Ventnor while Newport had connections to Ventnor via Sandown, Ventnor West via Merstone and to Freshwater. Significant users of freight services included coal merchants operating out of the trackside caves at Ventnor station. Quarry-related traffic at Shide chalk pit, Cement Mills, and Ashey Down quarry had ceased before 1950. Gasworks at St Helens and Newport, and the waterworks near Alverstone were historically connected to the rail system. The vestigial freight traffic that survived in 1951 was of particular interest as it tended to be the preserve of the four E1 tank locomotives.

By contrast the passenger services in 1951 demonstrated just how busy the network remained, even though it was on the threshold of massive closures. Thus, according to the working timetable dated 18 June 1951, the total passenger return trips operated each week ranged from 658 to 665, according to traffic demand.

Scheduled Return Passenger Trips (excluding empty stock and light engine movements), Isle of Wight – based on the Working Timetable effective 18 June 1951

Service	Mon-Fri (total)	Saturday	Sunday	Week (total)
Ryde PH–Ventnor	120	27	16–23	163–170
Ryde St J–Ventnor	5			5
Ryde PH–Sandown		9		9
Ryde PH–Shanklin		9		9
Brading–Bembridge	130	25	18	173
Ryde PH–Cowes	70	14	8	92
Ryde PH–Newport	5	1	3	8
Newport–Cowes			4	4
Ryde PH–Freshwater	5	1	1	7

Service	Mon-Fri (total)	Saturday	Sunday	Week (total)
Freshwater–Ventnor	5			5
Freshwater–Sandown	5	1	2	8
Freshwater–Newport	40	9	5	54
Cowes–Sandown	50	12	5	67
Cowes–Shanklin	5		1	6
Merstone–Ventnor West	40	8		48
Total passenger return trips	**480**	**116**	**63–70**	**658–665**

Description of the routes

Ryde–Ventnor

For the passenger, a journey on each of the island's rail routes was a series of quite distinctive experiences. For the crowds of holidaymakers en route to the resorts on the eastern and southern coast, it usually began with a brief transit of the Pier Head to Ryde Esplanade, followed by threading an urban setting before reaching the town's third station at Ryde St Johns Road, which was the location of a busy locomotive shed. Thereafter, the character of the line then became quite rural to Smallbrook Junction, where the former Isle of Wight Central route to Newport diverged to the west.

Brading, the junction for the short two and three quarter mile branch line to Bembridge, provided a passing place on the edge of salt marshes. Sandown, the junction for the nine and a quarter mile route to Merstone and Newport was inconveniently situated on the western edge of the town at some distance from the promenade. Shanklin station had the same problem, both stations possessing passing loops that were frequently used. Beyond Shanklin the railway forsook the company of the coast and climbed deep into the chalk downs towards Wroxall. On this section passengers on a heavily loaded five-coach train became aware of a slightly jerky motion, a reduction in speed, a growing crescendo of sound and an excess of smoke drifting past smoke the carriage window as the O2 tank struggled to surmount the Apse bank. Wroxall station with its adjoining hotel was decidedly rural in character, serving a small village amidst rolling downland where an up service from Ventnor would be encountered. Rugged upland country and a further climb was a prelude to the fume laden Ventnor tunnel, where smoke would often seep into the compartment through windows and doors before the train emerged from the stygian depths into the daylight and came to a rapid halt at the terminus in a the quarry-like setting, perched high above the attractive resort town. For the arriving visitor, it was always a delight to witness the locomotive taking water beside the telephone box before running rapidly around its train for the return journey. A further bonus was the sight of the town which occupied a succession of terraces culminating in the seashore far below. In an era when few traveled to continental Europe, it was easy to imagine that one had been deposited on the shores of the Mediterranean. Undoubtedly there was always a sense of occasion – the holidays were about to begin!

Brading–Bembridge

By contrast the Bembridge branch presented a blend of salt marshes and woodland punctuated by the gasworks and the slightly forlorn port facilities beyond the intermediate station of St Helens. At the quite impressive terminus the railway was a continuing object of interest in which visitors gathered to witness the ritual of running the loco around its train, using a turntable that could barely accommodate an O2 locomotive. It was a shorter distance by road between Ryde and Bembridge but the branch had a remarkably generous train service.

Sandown–Newport & Ventnor West branch

The Sandown–Newport line, had it survived, might in today's brand fixated world have been styled the 'Heart of Vectis

Line', for it pursued a delightful rural route following the headwaters of the Medina River, with views of the Downs to the north, towards Newport, the administrative centre of both the island and its rail network. Its six intermediate stations were at best described as being 'near to' small villages and hamlets. Merstone was something of an exception in that it was more remote from settlement but was the junction for the island's most rural and least used railway line.

Here the Ventnor West branch turned south and pursued a lonely course across sparsely populated chalk upland to the unstaffed stations of Godshill and Whitwell, before entering the St Lawrence or High Hat tunnel and emerging on a ledge along the undercliff at St Lawrence with panoramic coastal views unfolding to the south. As an unexpected finale. the line expired at its strangely quiet and forgotten terminus tucked away at an inconvenient western extremity of Ventnor. North of Merstone station, where trains passed at the island platform, both rail and river kept company to Shide where there was at one time a short spur line to a chalk pit, from which Stroudley 'Terriers' maintained a shuttle service supplying the cement mills north of Newport. From here the train passed the site of the early temporary Newport terminus of the line at Pans Lane, before joining the Ryde–Cowes route after a succession of viaducts. Newport station, the hub of the island railways, while not always pulsating with activity, offered continuous and satisfying diversions for the visiting railway enthusiast.

Ryde–Newport–Cowes

The former Isle of Wight Central route from Smallbrook Junction to Newport and Cowes (eleven and a quarter miles in length) was the secondary main line of the island in 1951. The route was pleasantly rural as far as the eastern outskirts of Newport. The first station of Ashey was notable in two respects. It was the junction for a short branch that served a racecourse and a quarry at Ashey Down. This siding was an early casualty and records indicate that it was abandoned in 1929. It was here too that unstable soil conditions necessitated the relocation of the platform before closure. Haven Street was, and remains, an unusual station and passing place embodying a bare island platform with separate station buildings. In more recent times it has witnessed a transformation from a quiet country backwater to a central tourist attraction of the preserved Isle of Wight Steam Railway, which now operates from a new interchange platform at Smallbrook Junction to a point to the east of the former station at Wootton. A unique feature of the latter was the location of its station offices within the arch of a road overpass. Beyond Wootton lay the relatively isolated, but quite substantial, station of Whippingham which was frequently patronized by Queen Victoria on her journeys to and from her holiday residence at Osborne House. Newport was very much the nerve centre of the island system and with its large station, loco shed and carriage and wagon workshops and sidings, where an array of vintage rolling stock was stabled. The southern approaches to the station were enlivened by the convergence of the Ryde and Sandown lines, a swing bridge over the Medina and the Newport gasworks. North of Newport the railway followed the west shore of the Medina to a cement works replete with its own employee's halt, a spur to the island's principal freight interchange at Medina Wharf, the 'suburban' station of Mill Hill and a short tunnel before the somewhat cramped terminus at Cowes was reached, tucked away in a side street.

Newport–Yarmouth–Freshwater

The 'withered arm' of the Isle of Wight rail network extended twelve miles west from Newport through thinly populated countryside to the tiny, but ancient, ferry port of Yarmouth and the village of Freshwater – the gateway to the Needles, the scenic west coast and literary associations with Tennyson. Although the Freshwater line had a truly branch line atmosphere it also had some interesting connections. The writer was a frequent traveler, runabout ticket in pocket on 'The Tourist' the through train to and from Ventnor which 'whisked', by island standards, the visitor non-stop across the heart of Vectis and onward through pleasant farmland between Newport and

Yarmouth, ignoring intermediate stations. Of particular interest on this line, was that rarity on British Railways, the private station at Watchingwell. Apart from alighting there himself, the author can only recall seeing two other people patronize this little known outpost, over many visits.

Isle of Wight Railways Basic Chronology

	Opening Date	Closure Date
Cowes–Newport *	16/06/1862	21/02/1966
Ryde St Johns Road–Shanklin	23/08/1864	
Brading–Brading Quay	23/08/1864	21/09/1953
Ryde Pier Head–Ryde Esplanade (tramway)	28/08/1864	1966
Shanklin–Ventnor	10/10/1866	18/04/1966
Ryde Esplanade–Ryde St Johns Road (tramway)	1/08/1871	1880
Sandown–Shide	1/02/1875	6/02/1956
Shide–Pan Lane (Newport)	6/10/1875	6/02/1956
Pan Lane (Newport)–Newport	1/06/1879	6/02/1956
Ryde Esplanade–Ryde St Johns Road**	5/04/1880	
Ryde Pier Head–Ryde Esplanade***	12/07/1880	
Brading–Bembridge	17/05/1882	21/09/1953
Ashey–Ashey Racecourse–Ashey Down Quarry	1884	1929
Newport–Freshwater (goods)	10/09/1888	21/09/1953
Newport–Freshwater (passengers)	20/07/1889	21/09/1953
Merstone–St Lawrence	20/07/1897	15/09/1952
St Lawrence–Ventnor (West)	1/06/1900	15/09/1952

* Stations at Wootton & Whippingham closed 21/09/53

** Replacing tramway *** In addition to tramway

Epilogue

The railways of the island are now either shadows of their former glory or rapidly receding memories treasured by senior citizens, but it is still possible to recapture the atmosphere of the fifties by visiting the Isle of Wight Steam Railway at Haven Street. Better still, a picnic at Ashey on a summer weekend can combine the vision of a convincing degree of steam power (particularly the last surviving O2 tank *Calbourne*) hauling pre-grouping rolling stock amidst appropriately sylvan surroundings. For those intrigued by the prospect of travel on superannuated tube trains on the Island Line rattling along the truncated remnant of the Ryde Pier Head–Ventnor line between the ferry terminal and Shanklin, this remains a quirky but nonetheless well-used alternative to bus travel.

Selected Bibliography

Railways in the Isle of Wight: PC Allen & AB MacLeod, Allen & Unwin, 1967

The Freshwater Yarmouth & Newport Railway: A Blackburn & J Mackett, Branch Line Handbooks & West Country Handbooks, 1966

The Railways & Tramways of Ryde: A Blackburn & J Mackett, Town & Country Press, 1971

The Great Isle of Wight Train Robbery: RE Burroughs, Railway Invigoration Society, 1968

Once Upon a Line, Vol 1: Andrew Britton, Oxford Publishing Co, 1983

Once Upon a Line, Vol 2: Andrew Britton, Oxford Publishing Co, 1984

Once Upon a Line, Vol 3: Andrew Britton, Oxford Publishing Co/Haynes, 1990

Once Upon a Line, Vol 4: Andrew Britton, Oxford Publishing Co, 1994

Isle of Wight Album: GM Kichenside, Ian Allan, 1967

Isle of Wight Railways Remembered: Peter Paye, Oxford Publishing Co. 1984

The Ventnor West Branch: Peter Paye, Wild Swan, 1992

The Isle of Wight Railways: Michael Robbins, Oakwood Press, 1953

Farewell to Steam – Isle of Wight: Matthew Wells, Rochester Press, 1985

Railways in the Isle of Wight: CJ Whittington, GG Saunders, no date

Acknowledgements

Thanks are due to two old friends, Jim Aston and Gerald Siviour for plugging gaps in my collection of Isle of Wight photographs. Michael Bowie of Lux Photographic Services, Carleton Place, Ontario continues his excellent restorative work on my fifty year old negatives. Last, but not least, I am indebted to Norman Johnston of Colourpoint Books for making this memorial to a fondly remembered railway system a reality. Unless otherwise credited, all photographs are by the author.

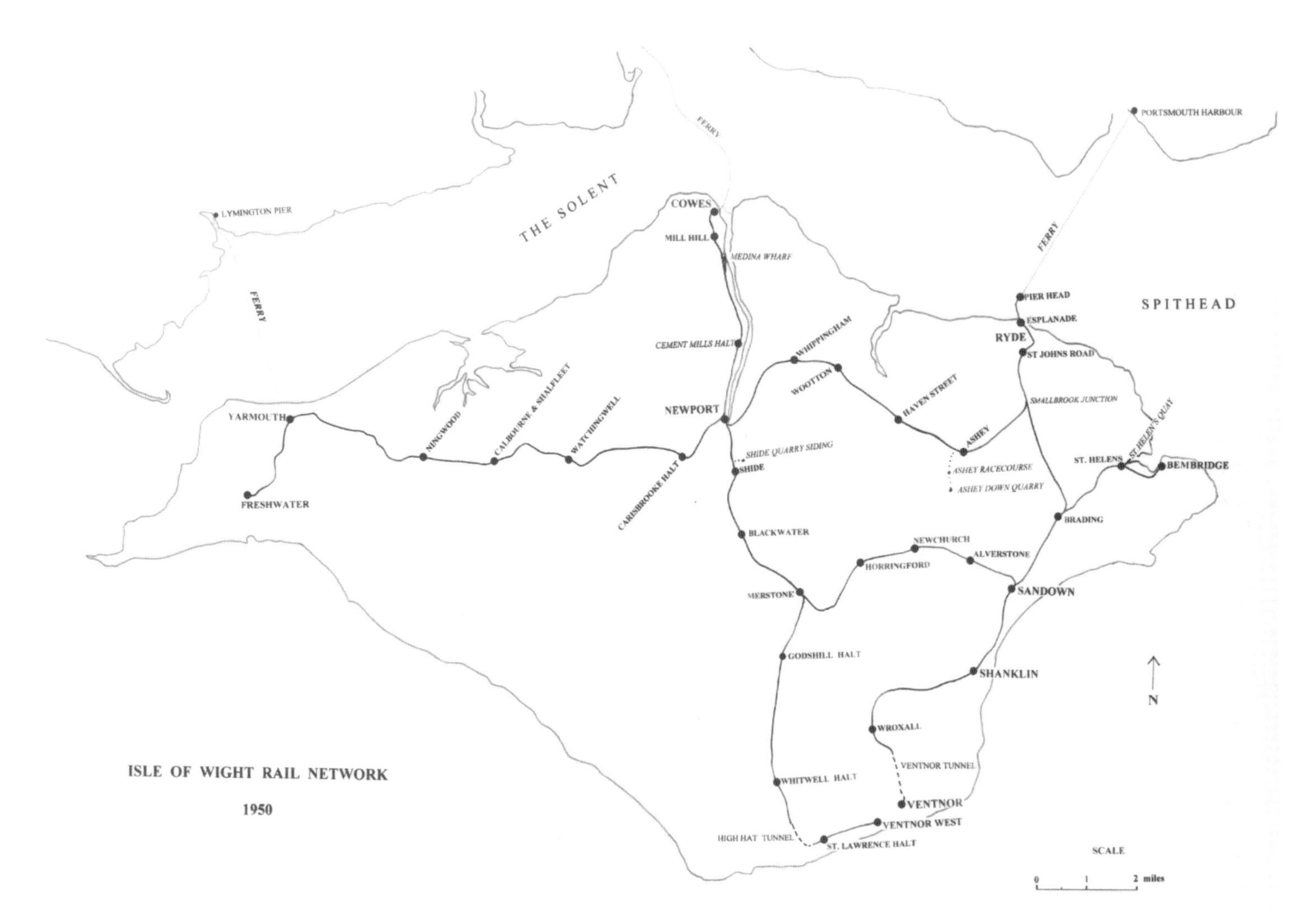

A flashback to another age in which the Isle of Wight was a preferred destination for English holidaymakers. 02 class 0-4-4T No 29 *Alverstone* leaves Newport for Freshwater on 28 August 1953. It is passing the site of an earlier station of the Freshwater,Yarmouth & Newport Railway with 'The Tourist', the only named train to operate on the Isle of Wight in the 1950s. This summer season service ran on Mondays to Fridays from Ventnor to Freshwater and return. It had the distinction of running non-stop between Sandown and Newport and Newport and Yarmouth. Running time, excluding intermediate stops at Wroxall, Shanklin, Sandown, Newport and Yarmouth, was about 69 minutes for the total distance of 27 miles The nine miles from Sandown to Newport were covered in 20 minutes which allowed for crossing a down train at Merstone. The junction at Newport faced in the direction of Cowes which necessitated a reversal for both departing and arriving trains on the Freshwater line.

No 25 *Godshill* gathers speed as it crosses the wrought iron structure of the Towngate viaduct after leaving Newport with a Ryde–Freshwater train on 27 August 1953.

Carisbrooke had declined in significance since 1927 when it was reduced to halt status. The passing loop was removed in the 1920s. The halt was inconveniently situated ¾ mile from Carisbrooke Castle which stands on the hill behind the station building. At one time Carisbrooke was recognized as the station for Parkhurst prison, located two miles to the north, whose inmates occasionally loaded wagons here. The village, seen here to the west of the station on 25 August 1953, was more conveniently served by bus in the fifties and few passengers patronized the halt. Note the site of the former loop and the surviving waiting room on the up platform. The station building was destroyed by fire after the line closed.

Calbourne & Shalfleet station was located one mile from each of the villages it purported to serve. In this view towards the west, on 25 August 1953, an interesting feature is the corrugated iron ticket office which began life as part of the FY&N station at Newport. The short siding continued to be used by a coal merchant at that time.

Historically, Calbourne was an important shipping point for milk traffic by passenger train. Some of this business persisted until the 1950s and, along with the local coal merchant, may well have rivalled passengers in terms of revenue generated. The siding is full of coal wagons in this view on 20 September 1953.

Deceptively timeless rural tranquility at Watchingwell. This view east towards Carisbrooke and that in the other direction, opposite, were both taken on 20 September 1953.

Watchingwell formerly known as Upper Watchingwell, was a private station built to serve the requirements of the Swainston estate and its tenants. In later days the station was available to all travellers. Trains would stop if indicated by distant signals located each side of the station and controlled by the ground frame on the short platform. Note that in the final years of operation the station house was occupied and tickets could be still be purchased there.

In the fifties, Ningwood possessed the last remaining (but regularly used) loop on the Freshwater line. The station differed from others on the line in that the station building was not combined with a residence. Instead, the stationmaster's house was located adjacent to the two arch road overpass, of which only one arch was ever used by rail traffic. Note the water tank at the Calbourne end of the up platform which provided one of two loco watering facilities on the Freshwater line. The gate on the right was the entrance to a siding serving the Seely estate until its removal in 1929. Although Ningwood was significant in its later years as a passing place, passenger usage was negligible. This view was on 24 August 1953.

Much of the Freshwater branch was characterized by a switchback gradient profile. Here O2 No 27 *Merstone* is heading downhill towards the site of Wellow Siding with a Newport–Freshwater train on 24 August 1953.

No 33 *Bembridge* leaves Yarmouth with a Newport–Freshwater train on 27 August 1953. Ahead lie the final one and half miles across salt marsh and through wooded country to the westernmost railhead on the island.

Yarmouth station stood on the edge of town about half a mile from the Lymington ferry slipway. In early days it possessed staggered platforms, a passing loop and a signal box and handled livestock traffic destined for the Lymington ferry and the mainland.

A farewell glimpse of trains at Yarmouth on the last day of rail service, 20 September 1953. No 31 *Chale* pauses before departure for Freshwater, giving the footplate crew an opportunity to exchange reminiscences with passengers who have just completed an unrepeatable journey.

An odd juxtaposition of good and bad news at Yarmouth station on that sad day.

Freshwater, slumbering contentedly on 26 August 1953, boasted the most imposing station building on the branch from Newport, although its single platform was something of an anticlimax. It had been extended by the Southern Railway in 1932 (note the change of level) to accommodate the six coach sets used from 1934 on 'The Tourist', the through train to and from Ventnor. By the 1950s the loco and carriage sheds had been removed. The signal box, reflecting typical Southern Railway cost consciousness, had done previous duty at the Newport FY&N station.

After arrival from Ryde, O2 No 30 *Shorwell* is running around its train at Freshwater on 24 August 1953, before the return run.

Eastbound trains on the Freshwater line normally ran bunker first. Here O2, No 29 *Alverstone* has just passed the water tower at Freshwater with a train bound for Newport on 24 August 1953.

We now retrace our steps to Newport to follow the line from there to Sandown. No 33 *Bembridge* arrives at the 173 feet long platform at Shide with a two coach train from Cowes to Sandown on 25 January 1956.

Shide station, with its small wooden signal box, was situated almost one mile south of Newport on the Sandown line where the main road linking the island capital with Shanklin crossed he railway. North of Shide there was formerly a siding complete with a short tunnel. It served a chalk pit which provided raw material for the cement works situated between Newport and Cowes. This shuttle traffic was entrusted to Stroudley terriers whose light axle loading was appropriate for the chalk pit sidings. The A3056 trunk road has now obliterated much of the former railway right of way north of Shide. This view is on 28 August 1953.

No 31 *Chale* arrives at Blackwater with a two coach train from Sandown on 25 January 1956. The original wooden platform here was partially replaced and extended in length to 242 feet by the Southern Railway.

The quiet hamlet of Blackwater was served by a neat brick station replete with oil lamps as seen here on 25 January 1956. In common with all other stations on the line it was staffed during operating hours due to the existence of a level crossing. From Blackwater the railway closely followed the course of the river Medina to Newport.

0-4-4T No 27 *Merstone* barely disturbs the tranquility of the water meadows as it slows for a stop at Blackwater with a Cowes–Sandown train on 28 August 1953.

Merstone, rebuilt as the junction for the Ventnor West branch in 1897, occupied a rural setting, the peace of which was regularly disturbed by the hourly passage of trains at the only island platform on the Newport–Sandown route. On this occasion, 25 January 1956, No 31 *Chale* was heading north while No 33 *Bembridge* powered the Sandown train.

No 25 *Godshill* pauses at the 301 feet long island platform at Merstone with a Cowes–Ventnor service on 5 February 1956, the last day of train services. In the foreground the former stairway to a frequently waterlogged pedestrian underpass was replaced by a ramp by the Southern Railway. Beyond the station, at the Newport end, there was an additional siding used for stabling the stock for the Ventnor West line until the demise of this service in 1952.

Running bunker first and bustling along with one of the hourly Sandown–Newport trains on 28 August 1953, No 24 *Calbourne* enters Horringford. Today this scene is no longer disturbed by the sights and sounds of steam as the trackbed has been transformed into a garden while the station survives as a residence.

Looking at Horringford from the opposite direction, but on 5 February 1956, we see the typically rural setting of this Isle of Wight station. Here the Newport–Sandown line clings to the banks of the River Yar, a tributary of the Medina and the main Newport–Sandown road crosses the line.

Unlike other stations on the Newport–Sandown line, Newchurch had lost its station house which had stood at the platform end by the level crossing. Its largely wooden platform was adorned by a later simple wooden building. Until the 1930s the siding here handled significant quantities of cut flowers, vegetables and sugar beets. A train pauses on 1 February 1956.

The valley of the River Yar was a wonderful place to savour rhe rustic charm of the island's railways. Against a backdrop of the Downs, No 25 *Godshill* enhances the timeless quality of the scene as it approaches Newchurch with a Sandown–Cowes train on 5 February 1956.

Appropriately enough, this is No 29 *Alverstone* leaving Alverstone with a Sandown–Newport service on 1 February 1956.

Judging by the generous provision of platform seats at Alverstone, this must at one time have been a busy station. The solitary siding just visible at the western (Newchurch) end of the station rarely saw goods traffic in the later years. This tranquil view is on 28 August 1953.

No 29 *Alverstone* rounds the curve on the 1 in 55 gradient up to Sandown with a train off the Newport line on 1 February 1956. The main line from Ryde to Ventnor is to the extreme right.

E1 class 0-6-0Ts were most frequently confined to freight duties during the later years, but there were exceptions. One such as the 4.10pm school train from Sandown to Newport. Here, E1 No 3 *Ryde* has been rostered for this working and awaits the call to duty at Sandown on 1 February 1956.

We now move north from Sandown to look at the Bembridge branch. Seen from atop a signal swaying in a brisk wind on 28 August 1953, No 14 *Fishbourne* rounds the curve near the junction at Brading with a train from Bembridge. With only a month remaining before closure, the track is showing the inevitable signs of deferred maintenance.

The name 'St Helens' evokes images of heavy industrial activity in Lancashire. In contrast, the lesser known St Helens in the Isle of Wight was the only intermediate station on the Brading–Bembridge branch and slumbers here on 28 August 1953. To the east of the station are reminders of a now vanished technology – a gasometer and small gasworks. A spur line serving St Helens Quay joined the branch beyond the gasworks, which was formerly connected directly to the quay by a short narrow gauge line. With the upgrading of Medina Wharf between Newport and Cowes by the Southern Railway, St Helens Quay declined in importance.

Alhough the terminus at Bembridge was conveniently situated in the centre of the community, the line quickly assumed a decidedly rural flavour amidst the meadows, marshes and golf links to the southwest of Bembridge (formerly Brading) Harbour. No 14 *Fishbourne* has just passed Harbour (formerly Howe) farm crossing with a Brading train on 28 August 1953.

Photographed on the same day, the attractive station at Bembridge station occupied quite a restricted site. It appears that, in spite of impending closure, goods traffic was not yet history. Sidings on the branch frequently provided a resting place for discarded rolling stock in the later years.

The O2 0-4-4Ts were a tight fit on the small turntable at Bembridge and the process of running around the train always attracted spectators during the holiday season. Here the driver of No 14 *Fishbourne* is performing feats of precision shunting for the assembled admirers on 28 August 1953.

With the exception of summer season weekends, the provision of passenger accommodation on the Bembridge branch could often be quite generous. No 14 *Fishbourne* is about to set out with a three coach train for the short return run to Brading on 28 August 1953.

Leaving the rural tranquility of Bembridge behind, we now move to the Cowes line. With an occasional irregular pant from its Westinghouse brake pump No 33 *Bembridge* simmers gently in the summer sunshine at the now vanished terminus at Cowes, before departing with a Ryde Pier Head train on 25 August 1953.

All is quiet on the station concourse at Cowes on 1 February 1956.

The station at Cowes occupied a cramped position on a steeply sloping street in West Cowes. The site has now been redeveloped and few vestiges of the railway remain. An elderly couple mount the hill without banking assistance on 1 February 1956.

No 24 *Calbourne* arrives at Cowes with a train from Ryde on the same day. The footbridge from Cowes has since been removed to Medstead & Four Marks station on the Watercress Line.

The penultimate station on the Cowes line was Mill Hill. The station, with its sharply curved platform, was situated just half a mile from the the terminus at Cowes at the southern end of a 208 yard long tunnel and was photographed on 25 August 1953.

Newport was a veritable hub of the island network with routes fanning out in four directions. In 1953 it was still quite a busy place, as epitomized by this scene in which No 32 *Bonchurch* pauses with a Ryde Pier Head to Freshwater train on 20 September 1953.

With the departure of the holidaymakers, a calm descended upon Newport station during the winter months. On the last day of service on the Newport–Sandown line, 5 February 1956, a smartly turned out No 25 *Godshill* is about to depart for the doomed route across the island.

Apart from its loco shed and workshop facilities, Newport station was the administrative centre of the island's railways. The offices occupied the first floor of the somewhat nondescript station building. It is seen on 5 February 1956.

Newport boasted no fewer than four platforms, of which one (on the right) was a bay platform for Freshwater services as seen from the north (Cowes) end of the station.However, no trains are in sight on 20 September 1953.

A shed scene to remember! No 33 *Bembridge* is flanked by E1s Nos 4 *Wroxall* and 3 *Ryde* (which stands under the hoist) at Newport on 20 September 1953.

Two O2s – Nos 36 *Carisbrooke* and 25 *Godshill*, erstwhile members of the class which formed the mainstay of island power in the fifties – stand at the north end of Newport shed on 5 February 1956. Note the wrought iron tracery which enhanced the appearance of the water tower.

Opposite top: No 33 *Bembridge* approaches Newport with a Cowes–Ryde Pier Head train on 20 September 1953. Note the fine array of upper quadrant semaphore signals, the repair shops on the right and the junction with the Freshwater line on the extreme left.

Above: A somewhat funereal gloom has descended upon Newport station in April 1968. Note the barrier blocking access to the abandoned Sandown line.

Opposite bottom: E1 0-6-0T No 2 *Yarmouth* approaches Newport, where sister E1 No 4 *Wroxall* is shunting, with a coal train from Medina Wharf on 25 August 1953.

The parting of the ways south of Newport station on 1 February 1956, showing the hand operated drawbridge over the River Medina and the lines to Ryde (left) and Sandown (right). The building on the left is the Newport gasworks. This site is now transformed and is occupied by the dual carriageway A3054.

Island railwaymen were notable gardeners and there was hot competition for the annual award of 'Best Kept Station'. In July 1965 the hotly contested trophy resided at Haven Street station.

GR Siviour

We now go west from Newport to look briefly at the line to Ryde. The bucolic but isolated country station at Whippingham was one of the least used on the island system although the hourly trains from Ryde to Cowes stopped there, if only to cross trains in the opposite direction. The loop was a later addition, being added in 1912 (36 years after the station was opened). Replete with its former royal waiting room, the station saw occasional moments of glory in the nineteenth century when Queen Victoria visited Osborne House (two and a half miles distant) on her regular visits to the Isle of Wight, via Stokes Bay and Ryde. Whippingham and its easterly neighbour Wootton were the first casualties on the Cowes line in the 1950s. Note the rarely used siding, which has all but disappeared under the grass on the left. The station was closed within a month of the date of this photograph – 26 August 1953.

No 32 *Bonchurch* pauses on the last day of passenger service (20 September 1953) at the deserted Whippingham station with a Cowes–Ryde Pier Head service. An unusual feature of the station was the very short down platform – the result of rebuilding after nationalization.

No 34 *Newport* makes a vigorous start from Wootton with a Ryde Pier Head to Cowes train on 26 August 1953. The cutting here was subject to frequent soil creep and evidence of stabilization efforts are visible. This problem was continuous and accounts for the location of the new Wootton station to the east, when the section from Haven Street was reopened by the Isle of Wight Steam Railway in 1971.

Wootton station was unique on the island in that its booking office and waiting room were located within an arch of the bridge carrying the road linking Wootton Common to Wootton village. This is the view towards Haven Street on 26 August 1953.

The Ventnor West branch had already been closed for a year when I visited the island in 1953. This is the forlorn scene at Whitwell, looking north towards Godshill on 2 September 1953, one year after closure of the Ventnor West branch in September 1952.

Also on 2 September 1953, Ventnor West station gently decays after closure, prior to the removal of track and the redevelopment of the site. This is the view from the stop blocks.

A flashback to 18 April 1949, when the Ventnor West branch was still open. A1X No 8 *Freshwater*, which was subsequently returned to the mainland, has arrived at Ventnor West with the branch train from Merstone.

JH Aston

New uses for old buildings, twenty years on. Viewed from exactly the same position as the preceding photograph, the station house at Ventnor West stands marooned amidst an estate of bungalows in July 1969, where the branch line from Merstone once terminated.

Finally, let us look at the Ryde to Ventnor line, part of which survives today as an electrified line. No 21 *Sandown* leaves Brading with a Ventnor train in July 1965. The former Bembridge branch platform was to the left of the signal box.

GR Siviour

The Southern with an offshore flavour. Approaching Ryde Pier Head in July 1965.

GR Siviour

No 25 *Godshill* tackles the hard slog from Shanklin to Wroxall with a heavy train in July 1965.

GR Siviour

No 21 *Sandown* is close to the end of the line in more ways than one as it departs Wroxall for Ventnor in July 1965.
GR Siviour

No 25 *Godshill* takes much needed refreshment within the hilly confines of the terminus at Ventnor. The claim made by the sign adorning the station building was already sadly out of date.

GR Siviour

No 30 *Shorwell* takes water at Ventnor before returning with its train to Ryde Pier Head on 5 February 1956.

GR Siviour